Communicating

GW00503898

with
the public ...

... a guide for those on the front line

Michael Kindred and Malcolm Goldsmith

4M Publications

4M Publications
20 Dover Street, Southwell, Notts. NG25 0EZ
Tel/Fax 01636 813674

First published by 4M Publications 1997

ISBN 0 9530494 0 X

Further copies may be obtained from 4M Publications
at the address and telephone number given above.
Discounts on 10 copies or more.

Printed by Roy Allen Print Ltd., 52a Westgate, Southwell, Notts. NG25 0JX
Tel: 01636 813304

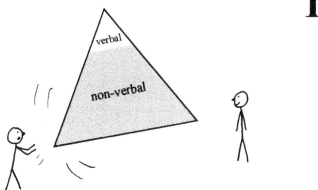

Most communication is roughly 90% non-verbal

- Some non-verbal communication is done consciously like shaking hands or pointing accusingly. A lot of it is unconscious like smiling or fidgeting. The other person will almost certainly be aware of it, even if you are not.

- In whatever way you communicate, verbally or non-verbally, the other person will pick up messages. These may not necessarily be what you intended to communicate.

- Paying proper attention to all these verbal and non-verbal signals is *active listening* and will be at several levels - listening to:
  - what they want to communicate.
  - what they are communicating without realising.
  - what they may be trying *not* to communicate.

Looks may say more than words

2

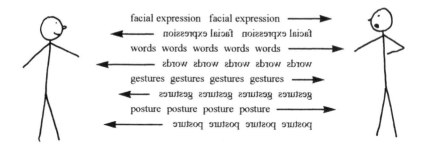

Two-way traffic

- When two people are communicating, each is involved in a complex process, even if one of them is doing most of the talking.

- Words, facial expression, gestures and posture have to be interpreted by both people. Some people are slower than others in understanding what has been communicated, perhaps because:
    - they feel physically ill or emotionally distressed.
    - they have impaired hearing and/or sight.
    - they find an accent or dialect difficult to understand.
    - their clarity of thought is impaired.
    - they do not speak the same language.
    - your words or jargon are not understood.

- Allow the person sufficient time to interpret what you communicate. Give yourself sufficient time to interpret their response.

- Don't rush in with your response before they've finished!

Time spent in careful listening can save time in the end

Take each person seriously

- When you meet someone for the first time, there is a lot of 'work' to get through. First of all, find out who they are, and let them know who you are.

- You need to establish why they have come. Is it:
    - to make an appointment?
    - to keep an appointment?
    - to make an enquiry?
    - to give you something?
    - to receive something from you?

- There may be problems to sort out ..... there may be a need for calming or reassurance. Whatever it is, *people need to be taken seriously,* for their own sake (and for the sake of any organisation that they may represent).

Everyone needs to be valued

4

Is your situation unnerving?

- The sight of uniform may make people anxious. For some people, seeing a surgeon, nurse, police officer or customs officer, for example, can be worrying or frightening. There will be some people for whom the opposite is true. For others, a person without a 'proper uniform', such as a tax inspector in jeans, can arouse anxiety.

- The way a room is arranged and furnished may make some people nervous or uncertain of where they should be.

- People may already be quite anxious and so perhaps you need to help them feel more relaxed.

- Remember: even when you are very friendly and helpful, you may seem quite intimidating to someone who is not sure who you are or what your particular job is.

Putting people at ease may ease communication

You may be difficult to understand

- Even if you both speak English misunderstandings do arise. Accents or dialects may cause difficulties. Ask the person to stop you whenever you use a word or expression which they don't know. Don't just say 'Do you understand?'. The person may say 'Yes' as an easy way out. Written material should be in the languages used by the community it serves.

- A person may not know why you are wearing a white coat, a black gown, official headgear, a badge or stripes on your sleeves - though not all at the same time!

- Your organisation may be unknown to people who use it. A person may have no idea what it does, what its purpose is, how it relates to other organisations or how it can help.

- Your everyday abbreviations or words (P45s, UB40s, registrar) may be puzzling to people from a different background.

Your organisation and words may be mystifying to others

6

Setting the tone

- If you start in an encouraging and helpful way, your dealings with the person stand a good chance of having a positive outcome. If you are abrupt or 'cold' then it may make it difficult for them to proceed further.

- Make sure you get names right - especially if they are difficult to pronounce. How you address someone is important. Tell them your name or wear a label - don't be the anonymous bureaucrat.

- Right from the start, believe that communication is possible, and if for some reason difficulties arise, don't give up. Try to find out what is going wrong, and work out ways of putting it right.

- Lack of eye contact may mean that the person is very nervous *or* that they are from a culture where lack of it is a form of respect.

- Smile!

A warm approach can help break the ice

Every encounter is important

- The person you are seeing may be one of many for you today but for that person this meeting might be crucial - and you may not be aware of that.

- Try to treat each person as the only one you are seeing today and give them your full attention. They will then feel that they have been taken seriously and heard.

- Remember:
    - they may have travelled quite a way at considerable inconvenience to see you.
    - they may have incurred expense which they may not really have been able to afford, such as train or bus fares.
    - they may need to get somewhere else on time.

- The more crucial the meeting is for them, and the more worried they are about the outcome, the more anxious they may be.

Make sure you mind and they matter

8

Are you playing power games?

- Communication usually works better when one person is not trying to:
    - dominate the other or be 'superior'.
    - appear more intelligent or be 'clever'.

- If you treat someone with respect - whoever they are - it is more likely that they:
    - will feel more at ease and confident.
    - will treat you with respect.

- Think about how you can minimise the feeling that you are the one with a lot of power and that the other person is powerless. For example:
    - could you encourage the person to make decisions for themselves wherever possible?
    - are there ways of listening and responding which could help to make the person feel on equal terms?

Respect can encourage people

Are you sitting comfortably?

- If you are sitting, are you slouched in the chair perhaps conveying boredom? Are you on the edge of your seat, maybe showing a desire to say something at the earliest opportunity? Are you sitting bolt upright, possibly denoting tension or are you sitting comfortably showing that you are relaxed and interested?

- If you are standing, have you adopted a relaxed stance, or are you portraying some kind of tension or desire to get some action?

- Is your stance appropriate to the encounter with the person?

- If you are having to make notes, have you a clean sheet of paper and a pen that works?

'Switch off' at home, not at work

10

Choose your words carefully

- Think about the words you use and how your sentences are formed. Are they words which the other person will understand? Have you used jargon or technical terms which will cause difficulties? Are the sentences easy to understand or are they rambling and long-winded?

- Think about the tone of your voice. Is it welcoming, kind, encouraging, accepting and caring or is it overbearing, harsh, cynical or rejecting? Does it sound as if you are being patronising and talking down to the other person?

- Think about the way that you emphasise certain words. Are you using this to help communicate more effectively, or are you putting the other person down?

Circumlocution and confabulation are diversionary!

Be clear about expectations

- As a starting point, clarify what the other person may be expecting from you - what do they hope to get out of this encounter?

- You will then be in a position to discuss whether or not their expectations are realistic. Try to do this in a way which shows that you care about what they have said.

- Don't encourage unrealistic expectations. For example, don't say 'There's no need to worry, I can easily sort that out.' if you are not sure. It is tempting to do this because you may want to impress people by your competence, or because you genuinely want to help them. Or you may be saying things as an easy way out of a difficult situation.

- At the end of the conversation, summarise what each of you has agreed to do.

If the goods are not for sale, don't put them in the window

12

Let people speak for themselves

- Let people say what they want - at their own speed. Don't try to rush them or complete their sentences for them.

- Allow people to explain things as they experience them - do not contradict them or keep correcting them. When they have finished you can ask questions for clarification.

- At the end of the conversation there may be 'different truths' or versions of the truth. Make sure you hear *their* understanding. It is rarely a contest between the two of you to establish the 'exact truth'. Differing versions may take a long time to sort out and other people may need to be involved. *What is important is that what is being said is being heard.*

- If someone appears to have a learning disability or is in a wheel-chair, make sure you address *them,* not someone who is accompanying them.

Communication involves hearing what people say

Labelling is for products, not people

- How often have you heard people say that someone is, for example, a nutcase, a raving hysteric, a moron, stupid or senile?

- Such labelling is unfair. Labels are offensive and are most probably assumptions not based on evidence.

- We should work on the assumption that we are dealing with rational, mature adults who deserve to be treated with respect and dignity. Even when our experience of someone tests this assumption to the limit, we should nevertheless give them the respect that any other person deserves. We do not know *why* they behave or speak in a particular way. If we were in their shoes we might be much worse.

- The desire to label someone usually springs from a lack of confidence on our part.

Mud can stick - keep communication clean

14

Don't be judgmental

- It is very easy to criticise people and to think that they are in the wrong and you are in the right.

- Being judgmental is likely to break down communication. Most people are not required to pass judgment on the people who come to them and it is far better if they don't.

- It is important that people do not allow their own convictions (perhaps they are prejudices) to have an adverse affect on the way that they deal with others. If someone wants to have ten children or green hair - then that is their choice - it is likely to be irrelevant to the matter which has brought them together.

- There *are* occasions when you may be right and the other person is wrong, but don't assume that this is always the case! If there is a difference between you, does this fundamentally affect the matter in hand? If it doesn't, don't allow it to get in the way.

Don't pass judgment, pass judgment by

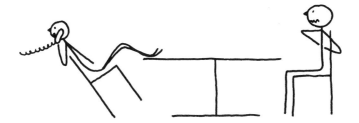

Handle interruptions sensitively

- When dealing with members of the public you should give them your full attention.

- Try not to be interrupted by phone calls or by colleagues. If this is unavoidable, apologise and deal with the interruption quickly. If possible, deal with the matter in a different place, out of sight and hearing of the person you are dealing with.

- Don't engage in personal conversations with someone who interrupts you, and *never* make comments about the person you are dealing with.

- If you need to telephone someone about the person you are dealing with, do it in their presence so that they know what information you are sharing; *or* do it in privacy after they have left. Don't do it in 'half-hearing'.

Crucial points may be missed if you are interrupted

16

Recognise hidden agendas

- The task you engage in when encountering a person is about 10% of what really takes place.

- 90% concerns 'personal emotional luggage'. Imagine how the following could affect your communication with someone:
    - you have had a row with a colleague and are very angry.
    - the boss has just given you a dressing-down, and you are feeling bruised.
    - someone you love is seriously ill.
    - you have just won a major prize on the lottery.

- The person you are seeing will also have hidden agendas. For example, they may have a worrying problem on their mind, or they may have had a difficult time the last time they came to your office/surgery/counter. They may also be embarrassed that they need to see you.

Try to keep your 'personal luggage' to yourself

People with disability

- *People with disability are people* (who happen to have a disability).

- Some people have a disability which is obvious, for example a person may be in a wheelchair. In other situations you may be aware of a disability only after a while, for instance a person may wear a hearing aid. Some people may have a disability which cannot be seen, such as dyslexia.

- Allow for the ways in which disabilities may affect the process of communication. For example you may have to take more time with someone who has impaired hearing or sight.

- Don't let the disability put you off - concentrate on what the person has come to see you about. You may feel uncomfortable - this is your problem which you should recognise. They are used to *living with* their disability.

People are people before they are anything else

18

The importance of confidentiality

- A person feels safer if they know that what they say will not be shared with anyone who does not need to know.

- If your job involves people buying tickets for a show from you, there would normally be very little information to be kept confidential. If you are a doctor's receptionist, then you may learn all sorts of private and personal details, so you will have a lot to keep confidential.

- If the firm or organisation you work for has guidelines laid down about confidentiality, then make sure you know them and abide by them. If it doesn't have any, should it have? If you do have to pass information on, be honest about this and explain why.

- Don't talk to colleagues about people you've seen, and what they have told you, unless it is a necessary part of your job. Similarly, don't talk about them to family or friends.

Only share on a 'need to know' basis

Dealing with emotions

- Communication can be difficult when strong emotions such as anger or distress are aroused.

- When emotions are aroused in the other person:
    - let them be expressed - the person may then calm down.
    - try to stay calm and be reassuring.
    - don't say 'I know how you feel' - responses which are not genuine are easily spotted, and no-one knows exactly how someone else feels.
    - if anger is expressed, don't assume that they are attacking you personally, and don't 'fight back'.
    - try not to get so emotionally involved that you fail to deal with what they came to see you about.

- When emotions are aroused in you:
    - try to regain your calm and try to focus on the purpose of the meeting.

Unacknowledged emotions can foul up good communication

20

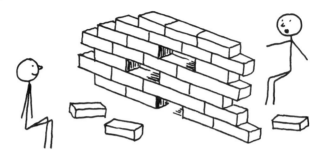

Talking to a brick wall

- Sometimes communication can be so difficult that you think you are talking to a brick wall. In those situations ask yourself:

  Is it me? Am I causing the problem, am I the blockage? Perhaps it's not the other person who is the brick wall. Maybe it's my inadequate understanding and inability to communicate. Does the other person feel that talking to me is like talking to a brick wall?

  Is it them? Are they feeling ill? Is someone or something troubling them? Do they find the process of communication difficult?

- Brick walls can be taken down brick by brick! So try to find out why the situation has arisen and where the difficulties lie.

Every wall can be dismantled

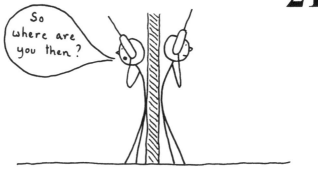

Using the phone

- Most people who deal with members of the public over the phone have been taught the standard way of opening up the call: a greeting followed by the name of the company or organisation, your own name and 'How may I help you?'

- Check if the person is ringing from a call box and is likely to be cut off, and don't leave them hanging on wondering what is happening if you have to leave the phone for any reason.

- If a person is rude or abusive be polite and speak quietly until they have calmed down. Dropping your own voice often stops shouting. Try to communicate that you want to help.

- Many of the things which apply to face to face communication also apply over the phone, the main difference being that there are far less non-verbal signals. You need to be particularly aware of tone of voice, intonation, emphasis and breathing.

Out of sight, but very much in mind

22

Drawing to an end

- Some people will find it difficult to accept that the time with you has ended. You may have to help them with this.

- Don't make it look as though you can't wait to get rid of the person now that *you've* finished.

- A handshake may be appropriate in some cases - but not in others.

- Don't use the same way of ending all the time - it can start to sound as though you are just repeating it parrot fashion. 'Have a nice day!' can become irritating.

- Make sure the person has all the information they require, and knows where they are going or what they need to do next. Make a note of any requests they have made and of what you need to do next as far as they are concerned.

Good endings can make for future good beginnings